Critical Theory: Challenging Truth and Reality

DR SHARON JAMES

This booklet is an edited transcript of a lecture delivered at The Christian Institute in April 2023.

Copyright © The Christian Institute 2023

The author has asserted her right under Section 77 of the Copyright, Designs & Patents Act 1988 to be identified as the author of this work.

Printed in May 2023

ISBN 9781901-086652

Published by:
The Christian Institute, Wilberforce House, 4 Park Road, Gosforth Business Park, Newcastle upon Tyne, NE12 8DG

All rights reserved

No part of this publication may be reproduced, or stored in a retrieval system, or transmitted, in any form or by any means, mechanical, electronic, photocopying, recording or otherwise, without the prior permission of The Christian Institute.

All scripture quotations, unless otherwise indicated, are taken from the HOLY BIBLE, NEW INTERNATIONAL VERSION®, NIV®. Copyright © 1973, 1978, 1984 by International Bible Society. Used by permission of Zondervan. All rights reserved.

The Christian Institute is a Company Limited by Guarantee, registered in England as a charity. Company No. 263 4440, Charity No. 100 4774. A charity registered in Scotland. Charity No. SC039220

Contents

5	Introduction: 'My feelings are more important than your facts!'
9	1. Critical Theory: Activism rather than Understanding
11	2. Key Thinkers and Movements
21	3. The Manipulation of Language: 'Social Justice' is not Biblical Justice
31	4. Five Pillars of Critical Theory
35	5. Impact on the Church
39	Conclusion: How should we respond? Confidence in an Age of Confusion
43	Further Resources

Introduction: *'My feelings are more important than your facts!'*

In September 2022, American politician Staci Adams declared:

> There is **no such thing** as a [foetal] heartbeat at six weeks. It is a manufactured sound designed to convince people that men have the right to take control of a woman's body.[1]

Many people would testify that hearing their unborn child's heartbeat was an unforgettable reality. It's biological reality too! A baby's little heart begins beating at around 21 days' gestation. Ultrasound enables us to hear the heartbeat by around six weeks.

But, because the issue being discussed was abortion, for Staci Adams the only relevant consideration was the power of the oppressor class (male) over the victim class (female). She would have dismissed any appeal to science as a power grab; a ploy to dismiss the plight of a woman with an unwanted pregnancy.

Increasingly in our culture, individual experience (more particularly the individual experience of those deemed to be oppressed) settles every argument and overrides objective evidence.

Just consider: a man doesn't have a womb and cannot give birth to a baby. But if you state that simple truth, you may in some contexts be accused of hate speech. A transsexual may have 'felt hurt' by your words. In any such situation, if the one claiming to be offended is from a 'victim class', their perception of the interaction is seen as more real than the intent of the person speaking. Their feelings cannot be questioned. Feelings are more important than facts.

Our culture is not only hostile to **biblical** truth – it is increasingly hostile to the very **concepts of truth and reality**. Dr Albert Mohler explains:

> ...we're now living in an age in which the secular world is unhinged from reality, unhinged from metaphysics, unhinged from truth, unhinged from being.[2]

That sounds alarmist. But Dr Mohler is right. And countless young people today are cheated of any certainty regarding truth or meaning. As Mary Eberstadt has said:

> They have been left alone in a cosmos with nothing to guide them, not even a firm grasp of what constitutes their basic humanity, and no means of finding the way home.[3]

"Not even a firm grasp of what constitutes their basic humanity!" Behind this breakdown of confidence in objective reality are the lies of the Evil One.

Lie one: There is **no Creator God**.
Lie two: If there's no God, there's no judgement, and **no absolute morality**.
Lie three: If there's no transcendent authority, who determines what's true at all? There's **no ultimate truth**.

All these lies are hardwired into a way of looking at the world that is described as Critical Theory.

The phrase 'Critical Theory' may sound academic; irrelevant to your life and mine. But although this worldview was birthed in academia, it has given rise to the culture of identity politics, and none of us can escape the effects.

That's why I have written this booklet. In the first section, I'll define Critical Theory, and take a look at some of the key thinkers and movements who have influenced this way of thinking.

Then, after commenting on the way that language is used to control the debate, we will take a look at the five main pillars of

Critical Theory, comment on how it has impacted the church, and consider how we should respond.

1. Critical Theory: Activism rather than Understanding

Critical Theory was a school of thought pioneered by a Marxist study centre founded in Germany in 1923, commonly known as the Frankfurt School. Its manifesto, ***Traditional and Critical Theory***, was written in 1937 by the first director, Max Horkheimer. In it, Horkheimer drew a distinction between traditional theory and critical theory.

Traditional theory refers to the traditional disciplines such as science, history and philosophy. These seek to **understand the world as it is**. They are about looking for truth and knowledge, and then about passing that knowledge on.

Critical Theory is not about **understanding** the world, so much as about **changing** the world. It's about **action**. It's about getting society to where it should be. It's about achieving **equity, or equal outcomes, or 'Social Justice'**. To get society there, all the institutions which prop up the status quo must be overturned.

The overthrow of society was conceived by the thinkers of this institution in **ideological** rather than physical terms. In other words, don't start by killing the powerful. Rather, persuade ordinary people of the terrible oppression they endure. They will do the rest!

Critical Theory represented something of a synthesis between Marxism (the call for violent revolution) and Freud's thinking (which would feed into calls for a moral and cultural revolution).[4]

Critical Theory was designed to **'enlighten'** people to see the way that **power structures** exploit them, especially those in minority groups. The aim is **action**, and the overthrow of structures, by spreading suspicion, mistrust and division. Encourage people to view **all authority as oppressive and all truth claims as suspicious**.

Summary:

*Critical Theory views variations in outcome in society as the result of **structural** injustice.*

*Some groups (identified as having privilege) oppress other groups (identified as those without privilege). Hence '**identity politics**'.*

*An individual may experience the oppression of living within **multiple** oppressed groups (e.g. minority race/sexual orientation/religion). Hence '**intersectionality**'.*[5]

*Critical Theory seeks to **awaken** us to the oppression endemic in the institutions of society and to move us towards **activism** to liberate oppressed groups. Those who are awakened and who engage in activism may be referred to as '**woke**'.*[6]

Critical Theory challenges hierarchies and institutions which exercise authority.

Critical Theory challenges claims to absolute truth.

2. Key Thinkers and Movements

If Critical Theory sounds abstract, it will help to look at some of the people whose ideas fed into this way of thinking. Space will only permit a short and selective overview. I provide more detail, and quotations from primary sources, in *The Lies we are Told: The Truth we must Hold*.[7]

Karl Marx (1818-1883): Religion is a false consciousness

Marx argued that religion exists because we are unhappy and alienated in our economic lives. It drugs people into acceptance of their lot. While living in London in the nineteenth century, he saw numerous opium dens filled with people seeking to dull their pain. He thought that this was a perfect metaphor for religion. Marx had been deeply influenced by the German anthropologist and philosopher Ludwig Feuerbach (1804-1872), who argued that God is a human projection.[8] The idea of God serves to sustain people through the hardships of life.

Marx considered every society to be based on an economic foundation (such as capitalism). The foundation is kept in place by institutions such as law, education, religion, the family and political bodies. All these need to be exposed as exploitative and pulled down. Revolutionary activism was the priority. Many Christians (and others) have naïvely read back into Marx their own desire to see greater economic and social justice. But Marx should be allowed to speak for himself. Please read *Das Kapital* for yourself. And then read an immensely powerful book by Paul Kengor, *The Devil and Karl Marx: Communism's Long March of Death, Deception, and Infiltration*.[9]

But our concern is Critical Theory, and we note that Marx

famously said:

> *The philosophers have only interpreted the world, in various ways. **The point, however, is to change it.***[10]

Activism takes priority over seeking truth. The first generation of Marxists pushed for violent revolution. Those associated with the Frankfurt School would promote *cultural* revolution. Later advocates of Critical Theory would attack Marxist truth claims. But a common motif recurs. Religion is a false consciousness that puts a brake on the activism that is needed to liberate oppressed groups. Religion must not be tolerated.

Antonio Gramsci (1891-1937): Overturn common sense!

A founding member of the Italian Communist Party, Antonio Gramsci,[11] reflected that Marxists had underestimated the power that bourgeois **values** had on working people. These values were passed on through the cultural institutions that preserved the status quo: schools, colleges, churches, the family, the workplace, governments and law courts. Gramsci described all this as the **hegemony**, from the Greek verb 'to lead'.[12]

He argued that the hegemony keeps ordinary people trapped in a false consciousness. It lulls them into complicity with a system which institutionalises inequality. The values formed by the hegemony are so embedded in Western culture that people think of them as **common sense**. Ideas which sustain this psychological oppression are passed down from generation to generation by the family, the church, schools, universities, law, the media, businesses, literature, science, and politics.

It seemed impossible that this whole cultural mindset could be overturned. Gramsci reflected that it would be a huge task to launch:

> *...[a] cultural movement which aimed to **replace common sense** and old conceptions of the world in general.*[13]

But he reckoned that the dominance of common sense could ultimately be toppled. A few determined people can achieve revolution if they succeed in changing ideas. Just start in the university lecture rooms. Then stand back and watch as those ideas spread through society.

Max Horkheimer (1895-1973): No God; no transcendent truth; we make our own reality

As already mentioned, a Marxist study centre was established in Germany in 1923.[14] A safe-sounding name, *The Institute for Social Research (IfS)*, was chosen. Historian Mark Sidwell describes this centre as:

> ...*an academic hothouse that was willing to think the unthinkable and reconceive Marxist theory, and whose intellectuals were also willing to imagine that the **best way to serve Western civilisation might be to destroy it**. . . [A] philosophy of **suspicion and negation** was pioneered by Mr Horkheimer in the 1930s and became the signature method of the Frankfurt School.*[15]

Underlying every aspect of thinking at the Frankfurt School was Horkheimer's conviction that there is **no transcendent reality, and no God**. The world of perception is a product of human activity. We make our own reality. Horkheimer coined the term Critical Theory, and hostility to Christianity is hardwired into this way of thinking. Truth, morality, justice, and ideas about universal human rights are **all** believed to be human constructs rather than transcendent and eternal realities. They have been framed in order to help sustain the status quo (or hegemony). There is no God. Humans constructed ideals such as 'universal rights' or 'free speech'. We can deconstruct them too.

Theodor Adorno (1903-1969): Freedom is dangerous

Theodor Adorno took over as Director of *IfS* in 1953. He and Max Horkheimer shared the conviction that the influence wielded by academia, the law, the church and the press in propping up the capitalist establishment could be undermined by Critical Theory. Their target was the whole framework of ideas upholding liberal Western societies. They were convinced that the problem with liberalism (free societies) was that people were **free** to sort themselves into hierarchies.

Societies need certain hierarchies of competence if the systems on which civilisation rests are going to function efficiently. But Adorno viewed all hierarchies with suspicion, describing them as *illusory harmonies*. People may imagine it is great for society to function efficiently. In reality, he insisted, the pseudo-stability of Western capitalism disguises the rotten reality. Multitudes are psychologically oppressed by inequality.

In order to end the oppression, the stability of society must be shaken. The ideas underpinning it must be challenged. You can do that if you undermine people's confidence in universal truth. Four steps can be identified:

Step 1: Persuade people that they're trapped in a 'false consciousness'

They may think they're happy, but they're not! They're being exploited by self-interested powerful forces. Horkheimer and Adorno co-authored *The Dialectic of Enlightenment* (1947), which argued that Western culture (films, music, radio and magazines) seduced people into accepting the establishment. They are trapped in a false consciousness and need to be awakened to their plight.

Step 2: Persuade people that the institutions that hold society together (family, schools, church, associations, government) are evil and exploitative

In 1950, Adorno published *The Authoritarian Personality*. The traditional family was presented as a repressive institution which brainwashed people into giving up individual liberty. It conditioned people into accepting authority, which made them susceptible to submitting to dictators. All traditional ideas about the family, religion and patriotism were presented as pathological. All authority, whether in state, home, school, church or the workplace was viewed as fascist.

Step 3: Undermine belief in absolute morality

Adorno redefined the concept of '**phobia**' (an irrational fear) to make it refer to moral disapproval of certain behaviours. He associated 'phobia' with **bigotry**. That was a master-stroke in manipulation of language. If you control the language you control the debate.

It became acceptable to assume that people who believe that certain behaviours are immoral have 'phobias' against people in minority groups. They act as an oppressor class, keeping the oppressed class down.

Step 4: Tell people that free speech is dangerous

What if some stubborn people continue to believe in absolute morality and ultimate truth? They cannot be tolerated. They must be silenced. Here, we turn to Herbert Marcuse.

Herbert Marcuse (1898-1979): Tolerance must be challenged

The German-American academic Herbert Marcuse spent time working for the Frankfurt School. He maintained that the ideals of Western civilisation sedated people into acceptance of their inauthentic place: cogs in the machine of oppressive capitalism. In his book, *Eros and Civilisation* (1955), Marcuse drew together the ideas of Marx and Freud to demand a non-repressive society, liberated from traditional moral norms. Demanding political liberation and sexual liberation proved to be a mesmerising combination, which fuelled many student protests during the 1960s.[16]

Marcuse's *Repressive Tolerance* (1965) claimed that the current state of society justified "strongly discriminatory tolerance on political grounds", including the "cancellation of the liberal creed of free and equal discussion".[17]

He argued that when people in power talk about "free speech" or "civil liberties", it is simply a ploy to protect their privilege. Minorities are powerless, so they must be given special privileges. This rebalancing is more important than civil liberties.[18] Revolutionaries understand this priority; others will need to be re-educated.

Jean-Paul Sartre (1905-1980): No forbidding is allowed!

Continuing the theme of "no God, no absolute morality", the existential movement made individual experience supreme. Each person is to seek their own authenticity.

Jean-Paul Sartre's *Existentialism is a Humanism* (1946) was based on one of his lectures. It summarises the key claim of existentialism.[19] Existence precedes essence. By "essence", Sartre alluded to the whole system of ideas, patterns and ideals governing individuals and society. He insisted that individuals shouldn't have to conform to the rules and expectations of anything outside themselves. We make our own rules; we define our own existence. We don't have to conform to the ideals of those around us as conveyed by church, family or other authorities.

There is no transcendent God. There is no external authority to dictate to us. If God does not exist, we are free. No forbidding is allowed!

Michel Foucault (1926–1984): Madness is freedom!

The same themes (no God, no absolute morality, and no ultimate truth) are all found in the work of French philosopher and author Michel Foucault.

Foucault set out to examine how people have thought about key issues through history. How have previous generations thought of sexuality, insanity or criminal justice? Foucault concluded that ideas have varied so much over time that **everything** is relative.

This brutally exposed the failure of the Enlightenment project, the liberal project and the modernist project. Any effort to answer all questions by unaided human reason will ultimately prove unstable.

When you deny God, the foundation of absolute morality and ultimate truth is fatally undermined.

Foucault's response was **not** to return to an acceptance of Divine authority. Rather, he pushed rejection of God to the absolute limit and blurred all moral and intellectual boundaries.

For example, *Madness and Civilization* (1961) shakes any confidence in what sanity actually is.[20] Can we say that there is such a thing as madness at all? What is reason? What is unreason? Who is to judge! Labelling some people as insane is simply a power play by the oppressor class to keep others oppressed. As we study the different ways of thinking of madness, sexuality or criminality, Foucault claimed that those who are in power arrange things and organise language in such a way as to protect their own position. For example, if people talk about marriage as the natural union of a man and a woman – that's using language in an oppressive way to demonise homosexuals, and keep heterosexuals in power.

Foucault's legacy is the idea that knowledge is a ploy used to keep the privileged in positions of power. Truth claims might be true or false, but how do we know? Truth is a cultural construct. We cannot escape from the fact that we may all be complicit in speaking in ways that express systemic power. We may be unconscious of doing this – but we are still guilty!

Foucault exploited others using his power and privilege, even as he castigated others for doing the same. He celebrated transgressiveness, regarded Christian morality as toxic, and lived out that liberation. He engaged in systematic sexual abuse of little boys aged between eight and ten while living in North Africa.[21]

And Foucault famously condemned institutions such as hospitals as authoritarian, mere "masks of bourgeois power",[22] by which doctors keep control of others. But when he was dying of AIDS, he was cared for with skill and compassion in *La Salpêtrière*, a hospital he had formerly condemned.

Rudi Dutschke (1940-1979): The Long March

I've mentioned the student protests of the 1960s. Rudi Dutschke, one of the student leaders in Germany, realised that violent activism had little chance of pulling down the establishment. In 1967 he came up with a powerful new slogan, calling for *Der Lange Marsch* or The Long March through the cultural institutions of Western society.

The students of the 1960s had grown up in a culture that said, "there is no God". They rightly sensed that people cannot live by bread alone.[23] Some of them rebelled against what Marcuse had described as the "hell of the Affluent Society".[24] But instead of turning back to God, their response was nihilistic. Smash down what's left! Let's enjoy absolute freedom and absolute equality amid the ruins![25]

Jean-François Lyotard (1924-1998): Bin the big stories!

In 1979, an academic called Jean-François Lyotard wrote a book entitled *The Postmodern Condition*. It had been commissioned by several universities in Quebec, Canada. Lyotard later admitted he had very little knowledge of the topic he'd been given. To compensate he had invented stories, and referred to books he had never read. He described this book as a parody, and his worst book.[26] But it was widely quoted. It promoted the idea that universal explanations, or "metanarratives", are ways of legitimising institutions of power. Instead, we should consult individual stories, especially non-privileged stories. The multiplicity of these experiences opens the prospect of multiple (contradictory) truths.

The virus of radical doubt and the death of common sense

We have considered some key thinkers and movements who contributed to the breakdown of confidence in absolute morality and ultimate truth. Yes, inconsistencies abound. There's no straight-line genealogy between them all. But what matters to us is the cumulative effect. During the twentieth century, first universities, then all the institutions of Western society, were invaded by the virus of radical doubt.

Intellectual elites increasingly dismissed truth claims as naïve, stupid, ignorant, even evil. The movement calling for deconstruction claimed that human language doesn't necessarily relate to objective truth at all. It's a series of linguistic signs, to be interpreted by the hearer or reader. This claim was usually clothed in such pretentious academic language that students were intimidated into thinking they should accept it without question. It's nonsense. Words do relate to objective truth.

But remember, the pioneers of Critical Theory had set out to destroy common sense. They regarded it as part of the false consciousness that upheld the hegemony. The task before them had seemed formidable. But what has happened to common-sense assumptions? How about the idea that a boy can't be a girl? Such common-sense assumptions may, today, be dismissed as illusions, or even denounced as heretical. That represents the triumph of Critical Theory.

3. The Manipulation of Language: 'Social Justice' is not Biblical Justice

In 2023, countless people go to work each day, scared of falling foul of Diversity, Equity and Inclusion Policies.[27] Using the wrong vocabulary could land them in front of a disciplinary hearing, accused of homophobia, transphobia or enbyphobia[28], or... what next?[29]

We cannot escape the reach of all this. It is the outworking of the various 'critical theories' that have emerged from Critical Theory. Some describe them as the unlovely offspring of the unholy union of Marxism and postmodernism.[30]

What matters to you is that your daughter may come home from school saying that she's really a boy. See there the reach of **critical gender theory**. You may get mugged, but you're not in a minority group, so your attacker may get a lighter sentence than if you were. That would reflect the leverage of **critical legal theory**. You may be the best-qualified person applying for a job, but the company has to meet Diversity, Equity and Inclusion targets. You don't even get an interview. That is an outworking of **critical race theory**.

Many people are deeply concerned about all this but dare not speak out. Many are intimidated into saying things they know to be untrue. They don't want to risk their job, their reputation, maybe even their freedom.

How have these ideas gained such an extraordinary stranglehold on so many people so quickly?

Control the Vocabulary: Control the Debate

We have already commented on some of the ways in which **language** has been manipulated to push people into questioning their assumptions. Those who are content in their family, church or job may be accused of suffering from '**false consciousness**'. They have been duped into going along with the status quo. By remaining passive, they are complicit in an unjust system. They need to wake up and recognise the reality of **structural injustice**, which keeps so many oppressed.

Many hesitate to question Critical Theory and its outworkings. *"Isn't it just about achieving social justice?"* they ask. *"As Christians, don't we want to see **more** social justice?"*

We need to understand that the single most powerful strategy adopted by the architects of Critical Theory was to hijack the word '**justice**', and subvert its true meaning.

The true meaning of justice is defined by God. **God is the God of Justice**. He demands that rulers rule with justice, according to the norms of his universal and perpetual moral law. He wrote his moral law on tablets of stone and placed it on every human heart. If everyone lived in accordance with the moral law there would be perfect justice. True justice must be understood within the framework of God's righteous and good character, reflected in his moral law, and also reflected in the conscience and natural law.

In a sinful world, tragically we do find exploitation and evil. Sometimes whole societies are characterised by gross injustice. Sometimes institutions are thoroughly corrupt. The strong do oppress the weak. Sometimes groups are discriminated against in various ways that result in multiple layers of suffering.

As Christians we **must oppose injustice**. Through church history we find followers of Christ speaking out for, and acting on behalf of, the oppressed and taking the lead in numerous campaigns for social reform. I trace that story in *How Christianity Transformed the World*.[31]

Such followers of Christ have been faithful to Scripture. Throughout the Bible, there are searing indictments of oppression and injustice. In a fallen world, God ordains that rulers should punish evil and promote good. He demands that they should judge impartially. All alike stand under the same law.

Upholding justice involves the protection of life and property. Without enforcement of the rule of law, there is no security of life or property, and no incentive to create the wealth that can lift families and nations out of poverty. In societies influenced by the biblical worldview, inequalities have been mitigated by the Christian virtues of generosity, compassion and social responsibility, as well as by a variety of reform movements.

But radical activists of the twentieth century viewed **all reform movements** as papering over the cracks of a hopelessly unequal civilisation. It **needed to be pulled down, not reformed**. The architects of Critical Theory denied the existence of God or any transcendent moral law. They viewed any inequality in society as intrinsically unjust. They **redefined justice** to mean equal outcomes. To secure equal outcomes involves taking away from those who have more to redistribute to those who have less.[32] This **injustice** is described as '**Social Justice**'.

'Justice' (according to 'Social Justice') means justice for groups. 'Guilt' in these terms means group guilt. People can be punished for the guilt of their group, even for sins their group committed in the far-distant past.[33]

When Christians hear the words 'social justice' we instinctively want to say *"Yes! That sounds great."* Many assume that it means equal access to legal rights, equal access to opportunities and opposition to unjust discrimination. But 'Social Justice' means the **opposite** of those things. It insists that some **groups** must have **more** access to rights and opportunities, and other **groups** must have **less**. It creates more discrimination. Social Justice is not Biblical Justice!

But hijacking the language of justice has deceived many

CRITICAL THEORY: CHALLENGING TRUTH AND REALITY | 23

into going along with the various **critical theories** which are destabilising society by dividing us into competing groups. Let's consider three of them.[34]

Critical Gender Theory: Queer Everything!

Remember, Critical Theory is about **action**. It's about moving towards a society where there is 'Social Justice' in terms of equity, or equal outcomes. So, what about the unequal societal outcomes between men and women?

During the 1970s, Women's Studies courses were introduced in many universities. The underlying assumption was that all social differences between men and women are the result of patriarchal oppression. Some radical feminists denounced logical discourse as 'male' thinking or even as the "rape of our minds".[35] Subjective (female) experience was argued to be more authentic. All previous thinking (including the Christian tradition and the Bible) was regarded as being infused with sexism. Anyone questioning this was branded as sexist!

This was not about 'getting fairness' for women. It was about destroying complementary male-female differences. Women had to be re-educated to realise that marriage and the family were an oppressive plot, devised by the wicked patriarchy.

Back in 1984, when my engagement to marry Bill was announced, a feminist colleague in my school staffroom was heard to comment derisively: "only toilets get engaged!" For a woman to promise life-long fidelity to a man, in her view, was a betrayal of the oppressed class of women.

What about women who claim to be happily married, or happy as mothers? They are the victims of 'false consciousness'. Such deluded women could be liberated by attending 'consciousness-raising' struggle sessions where they swapped stories of oppression and gathered courage to leave their families.[36]

Far better to get young women before they are trapped. Female students could be enlightened during women's studies courses. Mallory Millet, sister of radical feminist Kate Millet, described the impact of such courses:

> *Imagine this: a girl of seventeen or eighteen at the kitchen table with Mom studying the syllabus for her first year of college and there's a class called 'Women's Studies.' 'Hmmm, this could be interesting,' says Mom. 'Maybe you could get something out of this.'*
>
> *Seems innocuous to her. How could she suspect this is a class in which her innocent daughter will be taught that her father is a villain? Her mother is a fool, who allowed a man to enslave her into barbaric practices like monogamy and family life and motherhood, which is a waste of her talents. She mustn't follow in her mother's footsteps. That would be submitting to life as a mindless drone for some domineering man, the oppressor, who has mesmerized her with tricks like romantic love. Never be lured into this chicanery, she will be taught.*[37]

But soon, the category of 'woman' itself would come under attack.

Remember, Critical Theory is about breaking down 'commonsense' assumptions about what is normal. If there is no Creator God, and everything is socially constructed, then **gender** itself can be viewed as a social construct. If it is socially constructed, it can be deconstructed too.

Judith Butler (b. 1956) wrote *Gender Trouble* in 1990, in which she insisted that it is oppressive to say that anything is normal. Those who consider themselves as normal are the oppressors. Their assumption of normality must be stripped away.

Queer theory is all about destabilising normality. All boundaries need to be questioned. People need to doubt that there is any such thing as a fixed identity. Toleration is not enough! Everything, and everyone, must be 'de-normed'. To claim that *anything* is natural or normal may now trigger anger and bitterness.[38]

Critical Legal Theory

Remember that Critical Theory is about **action**. It's about moving towards a society where there is equity, or **equal outcomes**. Critical Legal Theory sees the law as a means to do that, and a means to remedy past injustice.

Traditional ideas of "equality before the law", and "Justice is blind", are regarded as means by which the privileged keep victims oppressed. Rather, law can be used to **compensate** oppressed groups for past and present wrongs.

In our therapeutic culture,[39] if someone thinks that their self-claimed orientation, or self-claimed identity, has not been respected or affirmed, it feels to them like actual violence. Words are seen as at least as bad as physical harm.[40] Police might drop everything to rush to the scene of an alleged "non-crime hate incident", because a tweet can "kill someone's sense of self". In Britain over a five-year period, the police investigated 120,000 "non-crime hate incidents".[41]

A property crime, on the other hand, could be regarded under Critical Legal Theory as rightful reparations. How did that person lay their hands on such a fancy car anyway? It's about time for the redistribution of resources! In 2020, activist Vicky Osterweil wrote a book entitled *In Defence of Looting*, in which looting is defended as "proletarian shopping", and property rights are claimed to be "innately, structurally white supremacist".[42]

If someone who commits a crime is deemed to be part of a victim class, their crime may be excused if it is thought to result from their disadvantage. Some attorneys in America publish lists of crimes they will not prosecute.[43] This is because the perpetrators are assumed to be from the victim class. Unsurprisingly, this has led to a rise in violent crime.

But if a crime is perpetrated **against** someone in a victim class, then the sentence can be heavier (it can be classified as a "hate crime").

Justice is no longer blind. We are no longer equal before the law. Theodore Roosevelt said that no one should be above the law, but no one should be beneath it either. All human beings should be afforded the dignity of individual responsibility.

Critical Race Theory

Racism is an ugly reality. Until 1967, interracial marriage was still against the law in sixteen states in America.[44] American author Shelby Steele (b. 1946) recalls that as a youngster, when he arrived with his dad in any new town, the first thing they did was find someone who could give them the inside story about accommodation, places to eat and other local services where they would not be turned away because of their skin colour.[45]

Racism is a sin. We are all made in God's image; we all have the same first parents (Genesis 1 and 2). As Paul says: "From one man he made every nation of men" (Acts 17:26). Therefore, the Christian view is that we should treat people with equal dignity and respect.

But Robin DiAngelo (b. 1956) and other advocates of Critical Race Theory seem to insist that treating people equally, whatever the colour of their skin, is dangerous. They view "colour blindness" as racist.[46] They insist that the priority is to secure reparative justice for **groups** of people who have, historically, been oppressed. There must be preferential treatment for such groups, in order to remedy inequity.

Black American author John McWhorter (b. 1965) argues in *Woke Racism* (2021) that Critical Race Theory pushes us towards seeing individuals first and foremost in terms of their racial identity. McWhorter resents the way that Critical Race Theory creates a culture in which his daughters are seen as "poster children rather than individuals".[47] He writes: "I consider it as nothing less than my duty as a black person to write this book."[48]

McWhorter's concern is well-founded. As Critical Race Theory makes its way into schools, children are directed to think of themselves **either** as victims, **or** as irredeemably guilty. In the zero-sum assumption that some groups are inexorably in racial conflict, children with parents of different ethnicities end up conflicted and confused.

Reni Eddo-Lodge maintains that the "vast majority" of white people have:

> *...never known what it means to embrace a person of colour as a true equal, with thoughts and feelings that are as valid as their own.*[49]

How, might one ask, can she possibly know? What of the many happy and successful marriages which cross ethnic boundaries? What are the children of such marriages supposed to make of such divisive teaching?

Robin DiAngelo insists:

> *...a positive White identity is an impossible goal. White identity is inherently racist; white people do not exist outside the system of white supremacy.*[50]

Many young people are being taught that white people can only really strive to be 'less white'. They cannot ever get it right in relating to people of other groups. DiAngelo suggests limiting smiling when engaging with people of a different ethnicity. Smiling, she suggests:

> *...allows [white people] to mask an anti-blackness that is foundational to our very existence as white.*[51]

Can you think of any better way to sow mistrust than by telling people ***not to smile***? You'll betray your racism if you do. But if you ***don't*** smile, won't that be seen as racist? To escape the no-win situation, some may find it safer to segregate themselves, and mix only with people of their own group. What a tragic betrayal of our common humanity!

Critical Race Theory stokes up anger, suspicion, resentment and division. It forces us all to focus on what divides us, rather than what unites us.

Those are just three of a number of critical theories. Space prevents dealing with others, such as Critical Pedagogy[52], or Post Colonial Studies.[53] But all the critical theories share common themes:

- *Critical Theory divides society into oppressor groups and oppressed groups*
- *The perception or lived experience of the oppressed groups can override objective truth*
- *"My feelings don't respect your facts!"*

Now we can stand back and take an overview of five pillars of Critical Theory.

4. Five Pillars of Critical Theory

1) Truth Claims are Power Grabs

Academics at the Frankfurt School denied the existence of God, and viewed religion as a false consciousness. If there is no God, there is no ground for ultimate truth. Without a transcendent authority, who, or what, is left to judge between competing claims to truth?

2) Universal Explanations are Suspect

The founders of Critical Theory denied any transcendent authority; we are left with the lived experience (or perception) of each individual. Someone may make a claim which is obviously contrary to reality. A woman can go into work and demand to be regarded as a man. And many will not dare to challenge her claim.

In some university departments, it is now said that objectivity is a "harmful research practice".[54] Authentic knowledge is achieved **within** different communities. People outside those groups do not have access to that knowledge. This is often referred to as standpoint theory. We might better understand it as the latest iteration of the old heresy of Gnosticism.[55]

3) Reason, Logic and Science are Tools of Oppression

Some say that science is a metanarrative that serves to uphold the establishment. They believe that straight white cis males from privileged Western societies invented logical methods of legitimising knowledge, in order to oppress other people.

Professor Rochelle Gutierrez of the University of Illinois claims that: "mathematics itself operates as Whiteness".[56] Asking to test truth claims by means of science or evidence is playing the game by rules set by the privileged. The tools used by the privileged (which could include science, rational argument, evidence) should be replaced with the lived experience of people in oppressed groups.[57] If one cultural group uses traditional medicine (including witchcraft or magic), demanding to test that medicine scientifically could be viewed as cultural oppression.

When Professor Garth Cooper, a distinguished scientist in New Zealand, objected to the idea that schools should give as much weight to Māori mythology as to science, he was placed under disciplinary investigation. His objection, it was claimed, could hurt the feelings of students and staff.[58]

Or consider the fact that scientific innovation can help deaf people to hear. Critical Theory, as applied to **Disability Studies**, interprets that as application of the bio-power of science to disrespect the **authentic lived experience** of a deaf person. Medical interventions to ameliorate the conditions of disabled people are viewed with suspicion. Those who choose to use those medical interventions may be seen as identity traitors.[59]

4) Don't Question my Experience!

In recent years, countless young people have been irreversibly damaged by gender reassignment medications and surgeries. Their individual perception of being in the wrong body has prevailed over the objective truth of biology. When we are not allowed to challenge anyone's experience, however bizarre their claims, a society is on the way to collapsing into unreason.

That's why Francis Schaeffer entitled one of his books *Escape from Reason*. He was alluding to Foucault's *Madness and Civilization*. Schaeffer paraphrased the take-home message of that immensely wordy book in the succinct sentence: *It is a fine thing to be crazy, for then you are free*.[60]

5) All Authority Structures are Repressive

Remember, the aim of Critical Theory is action in order to achieve equal outcomes. To get there, the institutions propping up society must be destabilised. Trust in authority has to be undermined.

After the Second World War, the righteous horror evoked by the uncovering of Nazi atrocities was exploited to stigmatise all authority as fascist. All authority figures, including teachers, parents, clergy, police, lawyers and politicians, were suspected of protecting the powerful and suppressing the powerless.

5. Impact on the Church

Under the cover of the deceptive phrase 'Social Justice', Critical Theory has been smuggled into all the institutions of the West, including numerous churches. It enters under the pretext of reform, but in reality it destroys. How?

1) Many have been persuaded to believe Christianity is the religion of the majority culture which has oppressed minority groups

This view rests on a re-writing of history (remember that Critical Theory is about mobilising activism, rather than seeking objective truth). It ignores the positive and transformative effect that the biblical worldview has had, not only on countries in the West, but worldwide.[61]

2) Critical Theory teaches us to assume that claims to absolute morality are offensive

Biblical morality is regarded as inflicting harm. Causing offence is viewed as inflicting harm just as severe as physical violence, maybe even more severe. Teaching on biblical repentance can offend people. Hence the demands for a wide-ranging ban on so-called 'conversion therapy'.

In the past, wrongs have been done in the name of Christ that did not reflect living Christianity. But the LGBTQIA+ movement insists that failure to celebrate every identity or sexual preference is bigoted and hateful. Affirming biblical morality is viewed as homophobic. It is tragic to hear church leaders apologising for 2,000 years of church history and apologising for Christ's own teaching ("a man shall leave his father and mother and be united to his wife and the two will be one flesh", Matthew 19:5-6).

James Lindsay, co-author of *Cynical Theories*, is an atheist. He warns Christian leaders that Social Justice (aka Critical Theory) aims to destroy Christianity from within. The language of Social Justice is used to guilt-trip well-meaning Christians. But when they are duped into endless apologies for the past wrongs they are told they have committed, Lindsay says brutally that they are being played as 'useful idiots'.[62]

Douglas Murray's book, *The War on the West*, also criticises many church leaders for naïvely surrendering to progressive demands. How foolish they are to continually apologise for how supposedly evil and oppressive the Church has been in the past![63] No surprise, Murray says, when the mob turns on the churches. In July 2021, in one week, thirty churches in Canada were torched. The head of British Columbia Civil Liberties association took to Twitter and said: "Burn it all down". One Canadian law professor described church burnings as "resistance to extreme and systemic injustice", and Prime Minister Justin Trudeau's top advisor said that burning churches "may be understandable".[64]

3) Critical Theory presents a False Gospel[65]

It has a **false view of humanity**. The Bible teaches that we are all equally created in God's image. Critical Theory sees us in terms of our group identity.

It has a **false view of sin**. The Bible teaches that we are all equally fallen: "In Adam all die". Critical Theory paints some groups as evil oppressors, others as innocent victims. The Bible teaches that each one, personally, will be held accountable to God. We should not punish children for their father's sin.[66] But according to Critical Theory, whole groups are condemned as guilty. One generation can be held accountable for the sins committed by previous generations and called on to pay reparations and make amends.[67]

It has a **false view of salvation**. The Bible teaches that all, equally, can find full and free forgiveness in the saving work of Christ. But according to Critical Theory, oppressor groups bear a sin that can never be satisfactorily atoned for.[68]

It has a false view of authority. Individual experience is placed over the Word of God.

Conclusion: How Should we Respond? Confidence in an Age of Confusion

Many evangelicals do not want to engage with what they call culture wars. They see it as a distraction from preaching the Gospel. "Just bring people to Jesus!" they say. It is tempting to keep quiet and try to avoid trouble. We do not want to cause needless offence. We do want to be sensitive to the experience of fellow human beings who have suffered appalling abuse and discrimination.

But the elevation of individual perception over objective truth is bearing bitter fruit. We have been put here for such a time as this! How should we respond? Certainly, we are to pray for a massive spiritual awakening. God does sometimes move in an extraordinary way to revive his people and then transform cultures. But we are also to be faithful and patient. Rebuilding the foundations may be a long-term project.

1) Don't be taken in by the claim that we should use Critical Theory as a 'useful tool'

Many today suggest that we should use some elements of Critical Theory to critique injustice.

Certainly, we should apply **critical thinking** to any question.[69] And we must challenge all injustice. But we don't need Critical Theory to help us to do that. We've already seen that true justice is defined by the God of justice and his eternal moral law. Critical Theory comes up with 'solutions' for injustice that only make things worse, because they undermine God's moral law, and contradict the creation mandates.[70]

Hostility to the idea of a transcendent God is **fundamental** to Critical Theory. It is built on the assumption that there is no transcendent "out there" authority. We each construct our own reality. That leads to the blurring of all distinctions between truth and falsehood. It ends up with the concept of multiple contradictory truths. It ends up with the claim that "my feelings don't care about your facts!" Do not be surprised, then, when in the Australian state of Victoria pastors who are accused of hurting the feelings of people who hear their sermons are called in for re-education and threatened with imprisonment under the conversion therapy ban.

I have referred to Critical Theory as a virus. That is because those on the inside use that metaphor themselves. For example, in *Women's Studies as a Virus: Instructional Feminism and the Projection of Danger*, the authors say that one of the aims of women's studies is to equip students to function as "'viruses' that infect, unsettle, and disrupt traditional and entrenched fields".[71] In fact, the metaphor perfectly describes all the various critical theories arising from Critical Theory.

Disney's classic song, *Never smile at a crocodile*, includes the line: "*don't be taken in by his welcome grin – he's imagining how well you'd fit within his skin!*" Remember that warning when considering the claims of Critical Theory, especially when clothed in the smiling language of Social Justice.

Don't think that if you smile back nicely, you'll be left alone. Author and journalist Andrew Doyle warns that to go along with the demands of Social Justice activists only encourages them to advance further claims:

> They will continue to deny biological reality and threaten you if you do not acquiesce. They will tell you that the kind of colour blindness advanced by Martin Luther King is a form of racism, rather than an exquisite goal worth pursuing. They will bully people in the name of compassion, promote division and

> call it progressive, and rehabilitate a new form of racism under the guise of tolerance.[72]

And, we could add, they want parents who teach their children about biblical morality to be criminalised. They want preaching that calls out sin as sin to be outlawed.

No amount of winsomeness will make them go away.

2) Teach biblical ethics and live out Christ-like care

Many today teach that it's 'loving' to affirm people in whatever they claim about their identity or desires. But the apostle Paul had severe condemnation for those who approve what is evil (Romans 1:32).

When the Abortion Act was passed at Westminster in 1967, many evangelicals stayed silent. They did not want to put people off the Gospel. They did not want women who had had abortions to feel hurt. But over the decades I've heard the sad stories of women who say: "why didn't anyone tell me I was killing my own baby?" Their lives have been blighted by endless regret.

As we oppose the lies, we feel only compassion for those who have been deceived by those lies. We are to love and pray for them. When we expose the lies, we must do so with gentleness and respect. There is no point winning an argument if we lose the person we are speaking to because of the manner in which we make our case.

In the unforgiving culture of identity politics, many are experiencing deep alienation and loneliness.

The body of Christ, by contrast, extends love, care, compassion, and concern. It honours God when our local churches function as Christ's body on earth, offering communities of love, joy and peace. The apostle Peter instructed believers in a hostile culture to live good lives, marked by good deeds (1 Peter 2:12). Such countercultural self-giving had a mighty impact during the first three centuries of the Christian Church. It still does today!

3) Be confident in God's good purposes

Critical Theory has undermined the foundations of our civilisation. At a time when so many capitulate and go along with what they know to be lies, we proclaim the glory of God's truth.

Many today are locked in pessimistic despair. They are living without God and have no hope in the face of death.[73] They lack confidence that we can know anything for sure, or that there is any real meaning in life. The unloosing of all moral norms has resulted in brokenness and pain. The claim that there is no God, no absolute morality, and no ultimate truth, ends in disaster for individuals and societies. As the great American thinker Michael Novak wrote:

> *To surrender the claims of truth upon humans is to surrender Earth to thugs.*[74]

By contrast, living according to God's truth leads to individual and societal flourishing. The Creator God is the ground of truth, reality, justice and morality (Colossians 1:17; Acts 17:28; Deuteronomy 32:4; Psalm 89:14). The only firm foundation for the defence of human rights and dignity is the truth that we are all created in God's image.

We are confident because we know that the light shines in the darkness, and the darkness cannot overcome it.[75] The Gospel offers forgiveness and healing to all. Christ's work of redemption achieved the unravelling of the curse in every respect.[76] He defeated all evil, when he rose from the dead and ascended to his Father's right hand. When he returns we'll see the final outworking of that triumph. All sin must be judged, either in the person of Christ, or in hell. Justice will be done. The earth will be renewed and restored.[77]

We have good news for all people, and for all creation. Jesus Christ is the Way, and the Truth, and the Life. He promises to all who come to him:

> *Then you will know the truth, and the truth will set you free (John 8:32)*

Further Resources

Books:

Allen, Scott David, *Why Social Justice is not Biblical Justice*, Credo, 2020

Doyle, Andrew, *The New Puritans: How the Religion of Social Justice Captured the Western World*, Constable, 2022

James, S, *The Lies we are Told: The Truth we must Hold*, Christian Focus, 2022

James, S, *How Christianity Transformed the World*, Christian Focus, 2021

Lindsay, J, *The Marxification of Education: Paulo Freire's Critical Marxism and the Theft of Education*, New Discourses, 2022

McWhorter, J, *Woke Racism: How a New Religion has Betrayed Black America*, Forum, 2021

Mitchell, J, *American Awakening: Identity Politics and Other Afflictions of Our Time*, Encounter Books, 2020/2022, Part 1: Transgression and Innocence

Murray, D, *The Madness of Crowds: Gender, Race and Identity*, Bloomsbury Continuum, 2019

Pluckrose, H and Lindsay, J, *Cynical Theories: How Universities Made Everything about Race, Gender, and Identity – and Why This Harms Everybody*, Swift Press, 2020

Sidwell, M, *The Long March: How the left won the culture war and what to do about it*, New Culture Forum, 2020

Strachan, O, *Christianity and Wokeness: How the Social Justice Movement is Hijacking the Gospel – and the Way to Stop It*, Salem Books, 2021

Tinker, M, *That Hideous Strength: A Deeper Look at How the West was Lost*, Evangelical Press, 2020

Articles:

Novak, M, 'Awakening from Nihilism: The Templeton Prize Address', *First Things online*, see https://www.firstthings.com/article/1994/08/awakening-from-nihilismthe-templeton-prize-address as at 22 March 2023

Sey, S, 'How to be a Racist', *Slow To Write*, 19 December, 2020, see https://slowtowrite.com/how-to-be-a-racist/ as at 4 April 2023

Sey, S, 'Do not grow Weary Rejecting Critical Race Theory', *Slow To Write*, 11 December, 2020, see https://slowtowrite.com/do-not-grow-weary-rejecting-critical-race-theory/ as at 4 April 2023

Sowell, T, 'Discrimination, Race, and Social Justice', *The Federalist*, 13 June 2018, see https://thefederalist.com/2019/06/13/an-interview-with-thomas-sowell-on-discrimination-race-and-social-justice/ as at 4 April 2023

Audio:

'Queer Theory Is Queer Marxism', video from *New Discourses, James Lindsay*, 11 August 2022, see https://newdiscourses.com/2022/08/queer-theory-is-queer-marxism/ as at 22 March 2023

'Ideological Totalism in the Woke Cult', video from *New Discourses, James Lindsay*, 27 February 2023, see https://newdiscourses.com/2023/02/ideological-totalism-in-the-woke-cult/ as at 4 April 2023

Videos:

'Is Critical Theory Biblical?', The Colson Center YouTube video, 22 April 2020, see https://www.youtube.com/watch?v=DAABuCC96tI as at 4 April 2023

'Diversity, Inclusion, Equity | James Lindsay', Sovereign Nations YouTube video, 27 October 2020, see https://www.youtube.com/watch?v=3jLNgLABuTw as at 4 April 2023

'Jordan Peterson - Diversity, Inclusivity & Equity', Rational Philosophy YouTube video, 22 November 2017, see https://www.youtube.com/watch?v=TqcRVmOpIbY as at 4 April 2023

'Helen Pluckrose on confronting Critical Theory | Solutions With David Ansara Podcast #32', David Ansara YouTube video, 28 November 2021, see https://www.youtube.com/watch?v=xCMUAz7pMA8 as at 4 April 2023

'The Virus of Critical Social Justice', video from New Discourses, James Lindsay, 12 June 2021, see https://newdiscourses.com/2021/06/virus-critical-social-justice/ as at 4 April 2023

'Dr James Lindsay & Helen Pluckrose | "Cynical Theories"', John Anderson YouTube video, 16 December 2020, see https://www.youtube.com/watch?v=XNx5jnNF1MQ as at 4 April 2023

Websites:

newdiscourses.com/

sovereignnations.com/

christian.org.uk/

counterweightsupport.com

heritage.org/crt

From The Christian Institute:

Many resources available at christian.org.uk including:

Gnosticism: the.ci/gnosticismbooklet

Identity Politics: the.ci/identitypolitics

Free to Disagree: the.ci/freetodisagree

Are Christians on the Wrong Side of History?: the.ci/wsoh

The Moral Law: the.ci/morallaw

References

1. RNC Research Tweet, 22 September 2022, see https://twitter.com/RNCResearch/status/1572742298168958977?utm_source=substack&utm_medium=email as at 17 March 2023
2. 'Facing the Intersection of Culture, Politics, and Religion in the Secular Age: A Conversation with R. R. Reno, Editor of First Things', Albert Mohler, 7 April 2021, see https://albertmohler.com/2021/04/07/r-r-reno as at 17 March 2023
3. Eberstadt, M, 'The Fury of the Fatherless', *First Things*, December 2020, see https://www.firstthings.com/article/2020/12/the-fury-of-the-fatherless as at 17 March 2023
4. One of the intellectuals associated with the Frankfurt School, Eric Fromm, aimed to provide, through a synthesis of Marxism and psychoanalysis, "the missing link between ideological superstructure and socio-economic base". See 'The Frankfurt School and Critical Theory', *Internet Encyclopedia of Philosophy*, see https://iep.utm.edu/critical-theory-frankfurt-school/ as at 17 March 2023
5. For more on intersectionality see, James, S, *The Lies we are Told: The Truth we must Hold*, Christian Focus, 2022, pages 136-138
6. This word, used originally in a positive way, has in recent years often been used in a pejorative way.
7. James, S, *The Lies we are Told: The Truth we must Hold*, Op cit, chapters 4 and 5
8. Ludwig Feuerbach, *The Essence of Christianity*, 1841
9. Kengor, P, *The Devil and Karl Marx: Communism's Long March of Death, Deception, and Infiltration*, Tan Books, 2020
10. 'Eleven Theses on Feuerbach quotes', *Good Reads*, see https://www.goodreads.com/work/quotes/16908093-ad-feuerbach-ludwig-feuerbach-und-der-ausgang-der-klassischen-deutschen as at 17 March 2023. These words were engraved on Marx's grave in Highgate Cemetery, London.
11. Gramsci set out to trigger a slow-burning, long-term, intellectual revolution which would undermine the presuppositions which propped up the establishment. In 1928 he was sentenced to 20 years imprisonment for revolutionary activity. While in prison, he compiled a series of reflections in 33 notebooks which would later have a significant influence, not least on the student revolutionaries in the 1960s.
12. Hegemony, from the Greek verb: **hēgeisthai** ("to lead"). One definition is: "the social, cultural, ideological, or economic influence exerted by a dominant group", see 'hegemony', *Merriam-Webster*, see https://www.merriam-webster.com/dictionary/hegemony as at 17 March 2023
13. Emphasis mine. Gramsci, A, *Prison Notebooks*, 1920-1935, quoted in James, S, *The Lies we are Told: The Truth we must Hold*, Op cit, page 107
14. After Hitler took power in Germany in 1933, the Institute was moved to Geneva in Switzerland, and then to New York City. It affiliated with Columbia University in 1935, was based in the United States during the 1940s, and returned to Frankfurt in 1951.
15. Sidwell, M, *The Long March: How the left won the culture war and what to do about it*, New Culture Forum, 2020, pages 46-47 (ebook), emphasis mine.
16. Sidwell, M, Op cit, page 46
17. Marcuse, H, 'Repressive Tolerance', Lecture at Brandeis University 1965, see https://www.marcuse.org/herbert/publications/1960s/1965-repressive-tolerance-fulltext.html as at 22 March 2023
18. Elder, A, *The Red Trojan Horse: A Concise Analysis of Cultural Marxism*, 2017, pages 75-76
19. 'Existentialism Is a Humanism', lecture given by Jean-Paul Sartre, 1946, see https://www.marxists.org/reference/archive/sartre/works/exist/sartre.htm as at 22 March 2023
20. Foucault, M, *Madness and Civilization*, Vintage Books, 1988. It is true that madness has been stigmatised, and the mentally ill have at times been dreadfully treated. But Foucault failed to point out that very often it was Christians who provided compassionate care, and who ultimately pioneered reforms in the way that the mentally ill were treated. James, S, *How Christianity Transformed the World*, Christian Focus, 2021, page 136
21. 'Reckoning with Foucault's alleged sexual abuse of boys in Tunisia', Haythem Guesmi for Al Jazeera online, 16 April 2021, see https://www.aljazeera.com/opinions/2021/4/16/reckoning-with-foucaults-sexual-abuse-of-boys-in-tunisia as at 22 March 2023
22. Scruton, R, *Fools, Frauds and Firebrands: Thinkers of the New Left*, Bloomsbury Continuum, 2016, pages 105-6
23. Deuteronomy 8:3; Matthew 8:4
24. Marcuse, H, *One-Dimensional Man*, Routledge, 2007, page 26 (available at https://libcom.org/files/Marcuse,%20H%20-%20One-Dimensional%20Man,%202nd%20edn.%20(Routledge,%202002).pdf)
25. See "Graffiti in Paris during the 1968 Student Uprising", James, S, *The Lies we are Told: The Truth we must Hold*, Op cit, pages 110-112, 114
26. 'Metanarrative', *New World Encyclopaedia*, see https://www.newworldencyclopedia.org/entry/Metanarrative as at 22 March 2023
27. See McWhorter, J, *Woke Racism: How a New Religion has Betrayed Black America*, Forum, 2021, page 5
28. Enbyphobia: fear, dislike, or hatred of non-binary people.
29. See Doyle, A, *The New Puritans: How the Religion of Social Justice Captured the Western World*, Constable, 2022, page 35
30. See Pluckrose, H and Lindsay, J, *Cynical Theories*, Pitchstone publications, 2020
31. James, S, *How Christianity Transformed the World*, Christian Focus, 2021
32. Cheryl Harris claimed that property is a construct of Whiteness (viz. systemic racism) and the right to private property should be suspended. See Harris, C I, 'Whiteness as Property', *Harvard Law Review*, June 1993 106(8), pages 1707-1791
33. "Social Justice" results in totalitarianism, for group rights are incompatible with individual rights. Balint Vazsonyi (1936-2003) lived under both Nazi and Communist regimes. He wrote: "*the Rule of Law and the Search for Social Justice cannot exist side-by-side because social justice requires that those who possess more of anything have it taken away from them. The Rule of Law will not permit that. It exists to guarantee conditions in which more people can have more liberty, more rights, more possessions. Prophets of social justice . . . focus on who should have less. Because they have nothing to give, they can

only take away. First, they take away opportunity. Next, they take away possessions. In the end, they have to take away life itself." That sounds dramatic. But Vazsonyi had witnessed the horror resulting when supposedly equal outcomes were enforced on whole nations during the twentieth century. See Vazsonyi, B, *America's Thirty Year War: Who is Winning?* Regnery, 1998, page 59

34. See James, S, *The Lies we are Told: The Truth we must Hold* for more on each of these three themes.
35. Western culture is based on the passing down of knowledge. We are created in the image of God. We have been endowed by our Creator with the rational capacity to explore and develop God's created order. But all previous 'logical thinking' was denounced as androcentric. Our whole culture (including the Christian tradition) is infused with a conceptual error of vast proportion, the androcentric (man-centred) fallacy. All human thought has been communicated from the male viewpoint and is distorted. All thought has to be restructured, beginning with a female perspective. The bias of male thinking, the "rape of our minds", must be eliminated. Lerner, G, *The Creation of Patriarchy*, Oxford University Press, 1986, pages 220, 225 (available at https://gepacf.files.wordpress.com/2015/03/women-and-history_-v-1-gerda-lerner-the-creation-of-patriarchy-oxford-university-press-1987.pdf). For more on radical feminism, see James, S, *God's Design for Women in an Age of Gender Confusion*, Evangelical Press, 2019
36. 'Marxist Feminism's Ruined Lives', *FrontPage Magazine*, 1 September 2014, see https://www.frontpagemag.com/marxist-feminisms-ruined-lives-mallory-millett/ as at 22 March 2023
37. *Loc cit*
38. 'Queer Theory Is Queer Marxism', video from *New Discourses*, James Lindsay, 11 August 2022, see https://newdiscourses.com/2022/08/queer-theory-is-queer-marxism/ as at 22 March 2023
39. See 'The importance of repression', *Unherd*, 29 September 2021, see https://unherd.com/2021/09/why-we-need-to-be-repressed/ as at 25 April 2023
40. McWhorter, J, *Woke Racism: How a New Religion has Betrayed Black America*, Forum, 2021, page 44. American writer Andrew Sullivan was named as 'icon' of LGBT History in 2006. But he insists that current progressivism has become as oppressive as any of the 'old' oppressions. He writes: *They seem to believe, and this is increasingly the orthodoxy in mainstream media, that any writer not actively committed to critical theory in questions of race, gender, sexual orientation, and gender identity is actively, **physically** harming co-workers merely by **existing** in the same virtual space.* (Emphasis mine).
41. Doyle, A, *The New Puritans*, Constable, 2022, page 36. As of March 2023, the Home Secretary, Suella Braverman, has instructed police not to record "non-crime hate incidents", see 'Police told to uphold freedom to disagree with same-sex marriage', *The Christian Institute*, 14 March 2023, see https://www.christian.org.uk/news/police-told-to-uphold-freedom-to-disagree-with-same-sex-marriage/ as at 31 March 2023
42. Osterweil, V, *In Defense of Looting: A Riotous History of Uncivil Action*, Bold Type Books, 2020, pages 4 and 16. "Looting rejects the legitimacy of ownership rights and property, the moral injunction to work for a living, and the 'justice' of law and order" (page). See also 'The Pinnacle of Looting Apologia', *The Atlantic*, 2 September 2020, see https://www.theatlantic.com/ideas/archive/2020/09/there-no-defense-looting/615925/ as at 22 March 2023
43. *The Daily Signal*, 24 February 2021, see https://www.dailysignal.com/2021/02/24/meet-george-gascon-the-rogue-prosecutor-whose-policies-are-wreaking-havoc-in-los-angeles/ as at 23 March 2023

44. South Carolina only removed from the state constitution the prohibition of racial intermarriage in 1998; Alabama only removed the law against intermarriage in the year 2000. See Piper, J, *Blood Lines*, Crossway, 2011, pages 203-204
45. Steele, S, *White Guilt: How Blacks and Whites Together Destroyed the Promise of the Civil Rights Era*, Harper Perennial, 2006, page 8
46. The assumption that lived experience overrides claims of objective reality pervades DiAngelo's *White Fragility* (2011). All white people are racist without knowing it. If they deny it, they betray their "white fragility" and are merely defending their unearned privilege. If those who are part of the oppressed class deny that they are victims, they have "internalized their pathology" and are acting as a pawn of the oppressors. See also comment in Doyle, A, *Op cit*, page 196.
47. McWhorter, *Woke Racism: How a New Religion Has Betrayed Black America*, Forum, 2021, page xiv
48. *Ibid*, page xv
49. 'Why I'm no longer talking to white people about race', Reni Eddo-Lodge, see https://renieddolodge.co.uk/why-im-no-longer-talking-to-white-people-about-race/ as at 22 March 2023
50. DiAngelo, R, *White Fragility: Why It's So Hard For White People to Talk about Racism*, Penguin Books, 2018, pages 149-150
51. *The Guardian online*, 16 January 2019, see https://www.theguardian.com/commentisfree/2019/jan/16/racial-inequality-niceness-white-people as at 22 March 2023. Quoted in Doyle, *Op cit*, page 196
52. Lindsay, J, *The Marxification of Education: Paulo Freire's Critical Marxism and the Theft of Education*, New Discourses, 2022
53. For more about this, see James, S, *The Lies we are Told: Truth we must Hold*, *Op cit*, pages 151-152
54. Doyle, A, *Op cit*, page 158. Objectivity is based on the belief that "neutrality on a subject is the best way to determine its facts . . . Even 'rigor' is considered harmful because it involves 'following an established research protocol meticulously instead of ensuring data are contextualized and grounded in community experience'".
55. See resources from The Christian Institute: 'Gnosticism', *The Christian Institute*, see https://www.christian.org.uk/resource/gnosticism/ as at 6 April 2023
56. *The Independent online*, 25 October 2017, see https://www.independent.co.uk/news/world/americas/teaching-maths-white-privilege-illinois-university-professor-rochelle-gutierrez-a8018521.html as at 31 March 2023
57. Lorde, A, *The Master's Tools Will Never Dismantle the Master's House*, 1984, (available at https://collectiveliberation.org/wp-content/uploads/2013/01/Lorde_The_Masters_Tools.pdf)
58. *The Spectator online*, 4 December 2021, see https://www.spectator.co.uk/article/why-punish-a-scientist-for-defending-science/ as at 31 March 2023. Professor Cooper is himself of Māori descent, see *The Spectator online*, 4 March 2023, see https://www.spectator.co.uk/article/why-im-sticking-up-for-science/ as at 31 March 2023
59. Pluckrose, H and Lindsay, J, *Cynical Theories*, Swift Press, 2021, page 170
60. Schaeffer, F A, *Escape from Reason*, IVP, 1968, page 70
61. James, S, *How Christianity Transformed the World*, Christian Focus, 2021
62. 'Paulo Freire and the Marxist Transformation of the Church', video from *New Discourses*, James Lindsay, 22 August 2022, see https://newdiscourses.com/2022/08/paulo-freire-and-the-marxist-transformation-of-the-church/ as at 22 March 2023

63. *After the Ball* by Marshall Kirk and Hunter Madsen was a handbook for gay activists published in 1989. The authors put forward a strategy for success: persuade well-meaning Christians to believe that they've always been oppressors. Get them to continually apologise for their group guilt. Naïve and well-meaning Christians go along with this. They imagine it will make them popular. They're wrong.
64. Murray, D, *The War on the West*, Harper Collins, 2022, page 193
65. The following three points are vividly and simply communicated in a video presented by Joseph Backholm: 'Is Critical Theory Biblical?', What Would You Say, The Colson Center, YouTube video, 22 April 2022, see https://www.youtube.com/watch?v=DAABuCC96tI as at 22 March 2023
66. Ezekiel 18:20
67. McDermott, G R, 'Misunderstanding Race and the Bible', *Public Discourse*, 20 October 2020 (available at https://www.thepublicdiscourse.com/2020/10/72125/)
68. Mitchell, J, *American Awakening: Identity Politics and Other Afflictions of Our Time*, Encounter Books, 2020/2022, Part 1: Transgression and Innocence. In this unforgiving climate, it is unsurprising to find people faking their identity in order to claim the lived experience of someone in an oppressed class. For example: *The Spectator online*, 24 February 2023, see https://www.spectator.co.uk/article/raquel-evita-saraswati-and-the-new-race-fakers/ as at 22 March 2023. If the deceit of such people is exposed, they are viewed as doubly guilty: part of the oppressor class **and** guilty of appropriation. As such, they can never be forgiven.
69. To conflate 'critical thinking' with Critical Theory is naïve and dangerous.
70. So, the 'solution' to sinful abuse of women must not involve seeking to abolish gender distinctions (i.e. God's creation mandate for man-woman marriage and family life, "fill the earth"). The 'solution' to poverty must not involve destroying the means of wealth creation (i.e. God's creation mandate to "subdue the earth" – that is develop the earth's resources for the blessing of humankind and the glory of God).
71. Fahs, B and Karger, M, 'Women's Studies as Virus: Institutional Feminism and the Projection of Danger', *Multidisciplinary Journal of Gender Studies*, February 2016, 5(1), pages 929-957
72. Doyle, A, *Op cit*, pages 304-305
73. Ephesians 2:12
74. Novak, M, 'Awakening from Nihilism: The Templeton Prize Address', *First Things online*, see https://www.firstthings.com/article/1994/08/awakening-from-nihilismthe-templeton-prize-address as at 22 March 2023
75. John 1:5
76. Colossians 1:20
77. 2 Corinthians 5:10; Acts 3:21; Romans 8:21; 2 Peter 3:11-13